Wild Essence

ENNEAGRAM MEDITATIONS THROUGH ANIMAL SPIRITS

WENDY VANDE VAN DE POLL, MS, CEOL

Spirit Paw Press LLC

To Tammy, Deb, Kerry, and Rick—

Thank you for walking this path—alongside the animals and the enneagram spirits. Thank you for embracing their wisdom, and for journeying into the depths of essence with open hearts. Your presence, curiosity, and trust in the process have made this journey all the more meaningful.

With gratitude and love for all the animals.

Contents

How to Use This Book

THIS BOOK IS DESIGNED AS A JOURNEY OF SELF-DISCOVERY THROUGH the wisdom of the Enneagram and the voices of the animal world.

It is an invitation to go beyond simply understanding your type and instead experience your essence through meditation, reflection, and intuitive connection with animals and nature.

STARTING WITH TYPE 7 RATHER THAN TYPE 1

You may notice that we begin with Type 7 rather than Type 1. This is intentional. Tammy Hendrix , LCSW who wrote the ground breaking book *You are More Than A Type: Embracing Wholeness with the Enneagram of Essence* teaches that:

The *Type 7 represents possibility, adventure, and the expansive nature of the soul—qualities that invite us to step into this journey with joyful abundance, then uncover our deep inner belonging and finally grounding ourselves into our gut center.*

. . .

Just as the hummingbird flits from flower to flower, tasting the sweetness of life, we begin here to remind ourselves that this process is not about fixing who we are, but about embracing the fullness of our being.

TO GET THE MOST OUT OF THIS BOOK, FOLLOW THESE STEPS:

1. Read the Introduction

The introduction will help you understand the deeper purpose of this book—how the Enneagram, animal symbolism, and meditation work together to reveal your essence. Read it with an open heart and allow yourself to approach this journey with curiosity.

2. Read the Meditation for Your Type

Each Enneagram type is paired with a spirit animal that reflects its core strengths, challenges, and lessons. As you read the meditation, immerse yourself in the imagery, allowing the words to guide you into direct experience rather than just intellectual understanding. There is no "right" way to do this. Simply notice what resonates, what stirs within you, and how your body and heart respond.

3. Explore the Writing Prompt

After each meditation, you'll find a writing prompt designed to help you reflect on your experience. Writing is a powerful tool for integration—it takes what is felt in the body and heart and gives it form. Set aside a few quiet moments to journal your thoughts, insights, or emotions. If nothing comes to mind immediately, trust that the reflection is still working within you.

ADDITIONAL TIPS FOR YOUR JOURNEY:

- You can read straight through or skip to the type that resonates with you most.
- If you identify with more than one type, explore those meditations and notice which feels most aligned.
- Revisit the meditations as often as you like—each time, you may discover something new.
- Approach this book not as a test, but as an exploration. There are no rigid answers here—only invitations to *remember who you truly are.*

Take your time, trust the process, and let the wisdom of the Enneagram and the spirit of the animals lead you home to yourself.

A Journey Back to Yourself

Welcome.

You are about to set out on a journey—not one that takes you somewhere new, but one that brings you back home to yourself. The Enneagram is more than a personality system, more than a way to understand behaviors or motivations. It is a path of returning. A path of remembering.

Somewhere along the way, each of us learned who we needed to be to feel safe, loved, and accepted. We shaped ourselves to fit expectations, to avoid pain, to carve out a sense of belonging. We built identities, adopted roles, and clung to what seemed necessary for survival. And yet, beneath all of this—beneath the striving, the guarding, the seeking—our essence has never left us.

Wild Essence: Enneagram Meditations Through Animal Spirits is an invitation to reconnect with that essence.

Through the lens of the Enneagram, we will explore the core motivations that drive us, the fears that hold us back, and the deeper truth that has always been within us through meditation and writing prompts. But this is not just about understanding your type—it is about experiencing yourself in a way that goes beyond words.

To guide you on this journey, we turn to the wisdom of nature—specifically, the animals that embody the soul of each Enneagram type. These creatures do not strive to be something they are not. They do not wrestle with self-doubt or seek external validation. They exist in full alignment with their essence, moving through the world with trust in their instincts, their presence, and their place in the great web of life.

- The Hummingbird drinks from the present moment, whispering to the Type 7 that joy is here, now.
- The Great Blue Heron trusts its own balance, mirroring the inner steadiness of the Type 6.
- The Owl watches with quiet knowing, revealing to the Type 5 that wisdom is already within.
- The Koi glides effortlessly, teaching the Type 4 that nothing is missing within them.
- The Whale swims through the depths, showing the Type 3 that their worth is already vast and whole.
- The Dolphin plays without fear, reminding the Type 2 that love is not something to be earned.
- The Horse moves with freedom and purpose, carrying the spirit of the Type 1.
- The Bison walks with unwavering presence, reflecting the grounded nature of the Type 9.
- The Mountain Lion stands with quiet power, embodying the strength of the Type 8.

Each meditation in *Wild Essence: Enneagram Meditations Through Animal Spirits* is designed to take you beyond the thinking mind and into direct experience—into the felt sense of your own presence, your own strength, your own truth. This is not about fixing yourself. It is not about becoming something more. It is about realizing that you were never broken in the first place.

So take a deep breath.
Let go of any expectations.
Step into this journey with curiosity, openness, and a willingness to see yourself in a new way.

You are not here to become someone different.
You are here to come home to yourself.

Together let's begin.

Warmly,
Wendy Van de Poll, MS, CEOL
Leading with a Type 6

The Quiet Mind

Walk the path of the mind—seek truth like a lantern in the dark, security like a steady ground beneath your feet, and freedom like the wind that dares you to fly—only to discover that the answers, the safety, and the wings were within you all along.

Type 7—First Step

Guided Meditation for the Type 7:
Essence and the Hummingbird

This meditation is designed to help the Enneagram Type 7 in you to connect with your true essence, beyond the need for constant movement, excitement, or distraction.

The hummingbird, a symbol of joy, presence, and the sweetness of life, will guide you toward the realization that fulfillment is found not in chasing experiences, but in fully embracing the present moment.

Type 7—The Hummingbird

SETTLING INTO STILLNESS

Take a deep breath in . . . and exhale slowly.
Feel your body relax, your mind quiet, your heart open.

There is nowhere else to be right now.
Nothing to plan.
Nothing to anticipate.
Simply be here.

Bring your awareness to your heart.
At your very core, there is a light,
A radiant glow—your essence.
It is not in the future.
It is not in the next adventure.
It is already here.

Whole. Complete. Enough.

Breathe into this light . . .
Let it expand within you, filling you with warmth,
Softening the restless energy,
Replacing it with a deep, peaceful joy.

You do not have to chase this moment.
It is already yours.

Now, imagine yourself in a lush, vibrant garden.
The air is sweet with the scent of flowers.
Sunlight filters through the leaves,
Casting golden patterns across the earth.

All around you, life hums with energy,
But there is no urgency here.
Only harmony.

You take a slow step forward,
Not rushing to the next thing,
But fully feeling the ground beneath you.
Fully tasting the air.
Fully alive in this moment.

A soft buzz fills the air.
A shimmering hummingbird flits into view,
Its wings moving so fast they are almost invisible,
Yet its body remains still, balanced, centered.

It moves effortlessly,
Not out of restlessness,
But from a deep trust in life's rhythm.

The hummingbird is not chasing joy.
It is drinking from it—one moment at a time.

It hovers before you,
Looking at you with knowing eyes,
And whispers:

Happiness is not ahead of you.
It is within you.
Joy is not something to chase.
It is something to savor.

Let those words settle into your heart.
Let go of the need to move to the next thing.
Let go of the belief that something more is needed.

Right here, right now, there is joy.
Not because of what is happening,
But because you are present enough to receive it.

The hummingbird flits to a flower and drinks deeply,
Savoring the nectar without rushing,
Without needing more than what is here.

You, too, can drink from this moment.
You do not need to escape it.
You do not need to fill it.
You only need to experience it fully.

Breathe in the richness of this moment.
Feel the fullness of this breath.
The sweetness of this life.

There is no emptiness to fill.
There is no lack.
Everything you need is already within you.

The hummingbird lingers for a moment,

Then zips effortlessly into the sky,
Not running away,
Not seeking something greater,
But simply following the natural flow of life.

And so do you.

Breathe deeply.
Feel the lightness within you,
The openness,
The stillness in your joy.

Slowly, bring your awareness back.
Back to your breath.
Back to your body.
Back to this moment.

And as you open your eyes,
Know this truth:

You do not have to chase joy.
It is already here.
You are already whole.
You are already free.

Type 7—Writing Prompts

WILD ESSENCE OF TYPE 7

1. The Joy of Presence:
The hummingbird teaches that joy is not found in chasing the next experience, but in fully tasting the moment. Reflect on a time when you felt completely present and content without needing to plan for the next thing. What did that moment feel like? How can you invite more of this presence into your daily life?

2. Sitting with Discomfort:
Type 7s often move away from pain or discomfort by seeking distraction or excitement. Think of a recent moment when you felt restless, anxious, or uncomfortable and wanted to escape it. What would it have been like to sit with that feeling instead? What might it have been trying to teach you?

3. The Fullness of Now:
Imagine your life exactly as it is, with no need to change, add, or plan

for more. Write about what already exists that brings you joy, fulfill-ment, and meaning. How does it feel to recognize that you are not missing anything—that the sweetness of life is already here?

Type 6 — First Step

Guided Meditation for the Type 6:
Essence and the Great Blue Heron

THIS MEDITATION IS DESIGNED TO HELP YOUR ENNEAGRAM TYPE 6 connect with your true essence, beyond fear, doubt, or the search for external security.

The great blue heron, a symbol of patience, balance, and quiet confidence, will guide you toward the realization that true safety and stability come from within.

Type 6 — Great Blue Heron

SETTLING INTO STILLNESS

Take a deep breath in . . . and exhale slowly.
Feel your body settle, your breath deepen, your mind quiet.
With each inhale, you gather strength.
With each exhale, you release tension.

There is nothing to guard against in this moment.
No threats to analyze.
No decisions to second-guess.
Simply be here.

Bring your awareness to your heart.
At your very core, there is a steady, radiant light—your essence.
It is not defined by fear or preparedness.
It is not shaped by external security.
It simply is.
Whole. Complete. Trustworthy.

Breathe into this light . . .
Let it expand within you,
Filling the space where doubt lingers,
Where uncertainty tries to take root.

You are not lost.
You are not without support.
You are already grounded.
Already strong.
Already safe.

Now, imagine yourself standing at the edge of a calm, quiet lake.
The air is cool, the sky painted in soft hues of dawn.
The water before you is smooth as glass,
Reflecting the world with perfect clarity.

There is stillness here.
A deep, unshaken presence.

You step closer,
Feeling the solid ground beneath your feet.
There is no rush.
No urgency.
Only this moment.

At the water's edge, a great blue heron stands.
Tall, poised, completely at ease.
It does not flutter in panic.
It does not seek outside reassurance.
It simply knows.

Knows when to wait.
Knows when to move.
Knows that stability is not found in certainty, but in trusting oneself.

The heron watches you, then steps gracefully into the water.
It does not fear the depths.
It does not hesitate.
With each step, it remains steady—balanced, calm, sure of itself.

It turns to you, as if to say:

You are stronger than your fears.
You are wiser than your doubts.
You are safe—not because the world is certain,
But because you can trust yourself.

Let those words settle into your heart.
Let go of the need for absolute security.
Let go of the fear of not knowing.
Let go of the belief that you must be on high alert to be safe.

You are safe.
Not because you control everything,
But because you are adaptable, resilient, and deeply supported by life
itself.

The heron takes another step, and you follow.
Not rushing.
Not hesitating.
Simply trusting.

You move with the grace of the heron,
Not forcing certainty,
But embracing the rhythm of life.

The still waters ripple beneath you,
But you do not sink.
You do not stumble.
You are held.

Each step builds trust.
Not in something outside of you,
But in the deep wisdom within you.

The heron pauses,
Looks back at you one last time,
Then spreads its great wings and lifts effortlessly into the sky.

It does not question whether it can fly.
It does not seek permission.
It simply rises.

And so do you.

Breathe deeply.
Feel the steady ground beneath you.
Feel the strength within you.
Feel the unshaken presence that has always been yours.

Slowly, bring your awareness back.
Back to your breath.
Back to your body.
Back to this moment.

And as you open your eyes,
Know this truth:

You are safe.
You are strong.
You can trust yourself.

And that is more than enough.

Type 6 — Writing Prompts

WILD ESSENCE OF TYPE 6

1. Trusting Yourself:
The great blue heron teaches that steadiness is not found in external certainty, but in trusting your own inner balance. Reflect on a time when you trusted your own instincts rather than seeking reassurance from others. What was the outcome? How can you build more trust in yourself moving forward?

2. Facing Fear with Trust:
Type 6s often anticipate potential dangers or worst-case scenarios. Write about a fear that has been holding you back—one that lingers in your mind and keeps you from stepping fully into life. What if you trusted that you could handle whatever comes? What would your next step look like?

3. Anchored in the Present:
The heron stands calmly in the water, adapting to the currents without

losing its footing. Close your eyes and take a few deep breaths. Write about what it would feel like to release the need for control and simply trust where you are right now. What support, wisdom, or strength is already within you?

Type 5—First Step

Guided Meditation for the Type 5:
Essence and the Owl

THIS MEDITATION IS DESIGNED TO HELP THE ENNEAGRAM TYPE 5 IN you connect with your true essence, beyond the need for knowledge, withdrawal, or self-protection.

The owl, a symbol of deep wisdom, quiet observation, and inner knowing, will guide you toward the realization that you are not defined by what you know, but by the vast presence and awareness that already exists within you.

Type 5—Owl

SETTLING INTO STILLNESS

Take a deep breath in . . . and exhale slowly.
Feel your body settle, your mind quiet, your breath deepen.
With each inhale, you gather presence.
With each exhale, you release tension.

Here, in this moment, there is no need to analyze.
No need to retreat.
No need to gather more information.
Simply be.

Bring your awareness to your heart.
At your core, there is a quiet, steady light—your essence.
It is not defined by what you know.
It is not shaped by how much you understand.
It simply is.
Whole. Vast. Complete.

Breathe into this light . . .
Let it expand within you, softening the walls, dissolving the distance.
You do not need to earn this knowing.
It has always been within you.

Now, imagine yourself standing at the edge of a vast forest at night.
The air is crisp, the sky full of stars.
The trees rise tall around you, silent and strong.
A deep stillness surrounds you—
A sacred space of observation, awareness, and truth.

You take a step forward, feeling the cool earth beneath your feet.
There is no rush.
No distractions.
Only you and the quiet wisdom of the forest.

As you walk, you sense a presence above you.
Perched on a branch, watching with luminous eyes, sits an owl.
It is still.
Unmoved.
Effortlessly aware.

The owl does not seek knowledge frantically.
It does not gather for the sake of control.
It simply knows.

It sees through the dark.
It understands without effort.
It trusts its own wisdom.

The owl spreads its wings and glides down toward you,
Landing gently nearby, gazing into your soul.
Then, without words, it speaks to you:

You are not your thoughts.

You are not your knowledge.
You are something far greater—something infinite.

Let those words settle into your being.
You do not have to hoard understanding to be safe.
You do not need to retreat to protect your energy.
Your wisdom is already within you.
And it will always be enough.

The owl bows its head, inviting you to follow.
You reach out and place your hand against its soft feathers,
Feeling its quiet power.

Then, as if weightless, you rise with it.
Not as a seeker,
Not as an outsider,
But as one who already belongs.

You soar together, above the forest, above the world of questions.
From this height, everything becomes clear.
There is no need to hold on so tightly.
No need to over-explain or prove.
You can trust yourself.
You can trust life.

The owl turns, guiding you back to the earth.
And as you land, you feel lighter,
More open,
More connected to the deep wisdom within you.

The owl watches you one last time, then takes flight into the night,
But its wisdom stays with you—
Not as something external,
But as something that has always been within.

You take a deep breath in . . . and exhale.
Slowly, bring your awareness back.
Back to your breath.
Back to your body.
Back to this moment.

Carrying this knowing:

You are already whole.
You are already wise.
You are already enough.

And when you open your eyes,
Know that you do not have to seek anything outside yourself.
Everything you need is already within.

Type 5-Writing Prompts

WILD ESSENCE FOR TYPE 5

1. Trusting Your Inner Wisdom:
The owl teaches that true wisdom does not come from hoarding knowledge, but from trusting what already resides within. Reflect on a time when you acted on instinct or intuition rather than gathering more information. What did you learn from that experience? How can you trust yourself more deeply?

2. Opening to Connection:
Type 5s often withdraw to conserve energy and protect their inner world. Write about a relationship or moment of connection where you felt truly safe and seen. What made that experience meaningful? How can you invite more of this connection into your life without feeling drained?

3. Expanding Beyond the Mind:
The owl sees beyond logic, embracing the mystery of the night.

Imagine stepping beyond your thoughts and into a world of pure experience—where you don't have to analyze or understand, only feel. What does this world look like? How does it feel to let go of overthinking and simply be?

The Heart's Truth

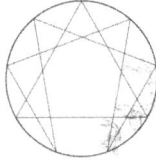

Live through the language of emotion—seek love to feel whole, significance to feel seen, and authenticity to feel real—only to realize that you have always been worthy, radiant, and enough just as you are.

Type 4—First Step

Guided Meditation for the Type 4:
Essence and the Koi Fish

THIS MEDITATION IS DESIGNED TO GUIDE THE PART OF YOU THAT relates to the Enneagram Type 4. Offering connection with your true essence—embracing your uniqueness while releasing the longing for something outside of yourself.

The koi fish, a symbol of transformation, inner depth, and resilience, will guide you to the realization that everything you seek is already within.

Type 4—Koi

SETTLING INTO STILLNESS

Take a deep, slow breath in . . . and exhale gently.
Feel your body soften, your heart open.
Let go of any tension, any longing, any weight you may be carrying.

Right now, in this moment, there is nothing you need to become.
Nothing you need to search for.
Simply allow yourself to be.

Bring your awareness to your heart.
There, within you, is a quiet, glowing light—your essence.
It is deep, rich, full of beauty.
It is whole.
It is not missing anything.
Breathe into this light, letting it expand within you . . .
It has always been here.
You have always been enough.

Now, imagine yourself standing by a tranquil pond.
The water is clear, reflecting the sky like a mirror.
The world feels still, yet alive with possibility.

As you gaze into the water, you see a koi fish swimming just beneath
the surface.
Its colors shimmer—deep gold, rich crimson, glowing pearl.
It moves with ease, unhurried, as though it knows its path.

This koi fish is your guide.
It does not rush.
It does not strive.
It simply moves with the currents of life, trusting that it is exactly
where it is meant to be.

It beckons you forward, inviting you to step into the water.
As you do, the coolness surrounds you, washing away any feelings of
incompleteness.
You are not lacking.
You are not missing something outside of yourself.
You are already whole.

The koi fish swims beside you, weaving through the water,
Reminding you that your depth is your beauty.
Your emotions, your uniqueness, your intensity—
They are not burdens. They are gifts.

As you glide through the water, you let go . . .
Let go of comparison.
Let go of the belief that something outside of you will make you whole.
Let go of the idea that you must be different to be enough.

You are enough.

You are not meant to be like anyone else.

Your essence is rare, like the koi,
Moving gracefully through life, embracing the depth of its own being.

The koi fish circles you one last time,
Then, with a final flick of its tail, it disappears into the water.
Not lost, but still present, still part of you.
For its lesson is now within you.

As you rise from the water,
You feel lighter,
Freer,
More yourself than ever before.

You do not need to chase something beyond yourself.
You are already home.

Breathe in that truth.
Feel it settle into your bones.
Let it become part of you.

And when you are ready,
Slowly bring your awareness back.
Back to your breath.
Back to the present moment.
Carrying this truth with you.

And as you open your eyes, remember:
You are already whole.
You are already worthy.
You are already deeply, beautifully, uniquely enough.

Type 4—Writing Prompts

WILD ESSENCE FOR TYPE 4

1. Embracing Wholeness:
The koi fish teaches that nothing is missing—you are already whole.
Reflect on a time when you felt completely at peace with yourself,
without longing to be different or elsewhere. What allowed you to feel
that way? How can you remind yourself that you are enough as
you are?

2. Expressing Your Inner World:
Type 4s often experience deep emotions that long to be expressed. If
your essence had a voice, what would it say to you right now? Write a
letter from your true self, speaking to the part of you that sometimes
feels unseen or misunderstood.

3. Finding Beauty in the Present:
The koi moves effortlessly through the water, fully immersed in its
surroundings. Pause and look around you. Write about the beauty that

exists in this very moment—in the colors, textures, sounds, or feelings present right now. How does shifting your focus to what is rather than what is missing change your perspective?

Type 3—First Step

Guided Meditation for the Type 3:
Essence and the Whale

THIS MEDITATION IS DESIGNED TO HELP YOUR ENNEAGRAM TYPE 3 connect with your true essence, beyond achievements and external validation.

The whale, a symbol of wisdom, depth, and presence, will guide you to the realization that your worth is not in what you do, but in who you are.

Type 3—Whale

SETTLING INTO STILLNESS

Take a deep breath in . . . and exhale slowly.
Feel your body settle, your shoulders drop, your breath deepen.
In this moment, there is nothing to prove.
Nothing to accomplish.
Simply be here.

Bring your awareness to your heart.
At your very core, there is a steady, radiant light—your essence.
It is not defined by success or failure, by recognition or results.
It simply is.
Whole. Complete. Enough.

Breathe into this light . . .
Let it expand within you, softening any tension, washing away any striving.
You do not need to earn this moment.
It belongs to you, just as you are.

Now, imagine yourself standing at the edge of a vast ocean.
The sky stretches endlessly above you, and the waves roll in a
rhythmic dance.
There is a deep stillness here.
A vastness that does not rush.

In the distance, a whale emerges from the water.
Its presence is ancient, wise, unshaken by the surface world.
It does not chase recognition, does not rush forward—it simply moves
with the rhythm of life itself.

The whale calls to you with a deep, resonant sound—
A sound that vibrates through your bones, reminding you:

You are enough, simply as you are.

It invites you into the water, into the quiet depths where striving
dissolves.
You step forward, feeling the cool embrace of the ocean,
And as you swim beside the whale, you feel its presence anchoring
you.

Here, beneath the surface, there is no need to perform.
No need to prove yourself.
Only truth. Only being.

You let go.
Let go of the pressure.
Let go of the masks.
Let go of the belief that your worth depends on what you accomplish.

You are worthy simply because you exist.

The whale moves beside you, effortlessly gliding through the deep.
It trusts the currents, surrenders to the flow.

It does not force its path; it simply follows the rhythm of life.

You, too, can trust this flow.
You do not need to push.
You do not need to chase.
You are already where you are meant to be.

Breathe that in.
Feel it settle into your bones.
Let the wisdom of the whale remind you—
Your worth is not in what you do. Your worth is in who you are.

And that is more than enough.

The whale begins to rise, guiding you upward.
Together, you break through the surface.
The air fills your lungs, fresh and free.

You are lighter now.
Freer.
Whole.

As you step back onto the shore,
You carry the stillness of the deep within you.
The wisdom of the whale remains, whispering through your soul—

You are already whole.
You are already worthy.
You are already free.

Slowly, bring your awareness back.
Back to your breath.
Back to this moment.
Carrying this truth with you.

And when you open your eyes,
Know that you do not need to become anything.
You only need to be.

And that is enough.

Type 3—Writing Prompts

WILD ESSENCE FOR TYPE 3

1. Worth Beyond Achievement:
The whale teaches that true worth is not earned through accomplishments but is vast and unshakable, just like the ocean itself. Reflect on a time when you felt valuable simply for being yourself, not for what you achieved. How can you remind yourself that you are already enough, even when you are not striving?

2. Removing the Mask:
Type 3s often adapt to what is expected of them, sometimes losing sight of their true self beneath ambition and external validation. If you could set aside all roles and expectations, who would you be? Describe your essence—not in terms of what you do, but in terms of who you are at your core.

3. Resting in Presence:
The whale moves through the depths with grace, unhurried and at ease.

Imagine a world where you don't have to prove anything to anyone—where you can simply exist, fully present in this moment. What would that feel like? How can you create space in your life to rest, breathe, and be without striving?

Type 2—First Step

Guided Meditation for the Type 2:
Essence and the Dolphin

Here is a guided meditation for your Enneagram Type 2, focused on connecting you with the essence and the dolphin.

This meditation helps the listener release the belief that they must earn love and instead embrace the unconditional love that already exists within them.

Type 2—Dolphin

SETTLING INTO STILLNESS

Take a deep, slow breath in . . . and exhale gently.
Feel your body soften, your heart open.
Let go of any tension, any weight you may be carrying for others.

Right now, in this moment, there is nothing you need to do.
Nothing you need to give.
Simply allow yourself to be.

Bring your awareness to your heart.
There, within you, is a warm, golden light—your essence.
It has always been here.

It is love, not because of what you do, but because of who you are.

Breathe into this light, letting it expand within you . . . filling every part of you.
You are already enough.

You are already loved.

Now, imagine yourself standing at the edge of a vast ocean.
The waves gently kiss the shore, inviting you in.
The sunlight dances across the water, shimmering like liquid gold.

In the distance, you see a dolphin leaping joyfully from the sea.
Its movement is effortless, playful, free.
It does not ask permission to take up space.
It does not seek approval.
It simply is.

The dolphin swims toward you, its presence radiating warmth and connection.
It gazes at you with deep knowing, as if it sees straight into your soul.
Then, with a flick of its tail, it invites you to enter the water.

You step forward, feeling the ocean embrace you.
The water is warm, weightless, holding you with perfect ease.

The dolphin circles you gently, reminding you of the joy of connection, the beauty of trust, the gift of love that asks for nothing in return.
It whispers to you:

You are loved. Not for what you give. Not for what you do. You are loved . . . simply because you exist.

Breathe that in.
Let it settle deep within your heart.
Love is not something you must earn.
Love is your birthright.

Now, the dolphin nudges you forward, inviting you to move with it.
You follow, gliding effortlessly through the water, letting go of resistance.

Letting go of the belief that love must be worked for, that you must prove yourself to be worthy.

With each stroke, you release old burdens—
The need to please,
The fear of being unwanted,
The belief that your value is tied to how much you give.

Instead, you embrace the truth:
You are loved. You are whole. You are free.

The dolphin leaps, and you laugh, feeling a lightness within you.
There is no striving here.
No fixing.
Only being.

You float in the ocean's gentle embrace,
Surrounded by love, held by life itself.

Let this truth fill you:
You are worthy. You are loved. You are enough.

Breathe it in.
Feel it settle into your soul.

And when you are ready, slowly bring your awareness back.
Back to your breath.
Back to the present moment.
Carrying this feeling, this knowing, this deep truth with you.

And as you open your eyes, remember:
You are not loved for what you do.
You are loved for who you are.
And that is more than enough.

Type 2-Writing Prompts

WILD ESSENCE FOR TYPE 2

1. Receiving Without Giving:
The dolphin teaches that love is not something you have to earn—it is
something you already are. Reflect on a time when you received love
or support without having to give anything in return. How did it feel?
How can you allow yourself to receive more freely in your daily life?

2. Loving Yourself First:
Type 2s often prioritize others' needs over their own. Write a letter to
yourself, filled with the same kindness, encouragement, and love that
you so easily give to others. What do you need to hear? What would it
feel like to care for yourself as deeply as you care for those
around you?

3. Being Enough as You Are:
The dolphin moves through the water effortlessly, without needing to
prove its worth. Imagine waking up tomorrow with the deep under-

standing that you are already enough, just as you are—without having to help, fix, or care for anyone else. What would change? How would you move through your day differently?

The Grounded Self

Move through life with instinct as your compass—seek control to feel safe, autonomy to feel strong, and harmony to feel at peace. Discover that true power comes not from resistance, but from trusting the deep, unshakable wisdom already within you.

Type 1—First Step

Guided Meditation for the Type 1:
Essence and the Horse

HERE IS A GUIDED MEDITATION FOR AN ENNEAGRAM TYPE 1, DESIGNED to help you connect your essence and the symbolism of the horse.

It focuses on releasing inner criticism, embracing wholeness, and flowing with life's natural rhythms.

Type 1—Horse

SETTLING INTO STILLNESS

Take a deep breath in . . . and slowly exhale.
Feel your body settle, your spine elongating, your shoulders softening.
With each breath, allow the tension of the day to dissolve.

Now, bring your awareness to your gut.
Within you, at your very core, is a quiet, radiant light—your essence.
This is the part of you that is whole, pure, and unshaken by the world's imperfections.
Breathe into this light . . . feeling it expand with each inhale.
Let it fill you with warmth, acceptance, and peace.

You have always carried this essence within you.
It is not something you need to strive for, not something you must perfect.
It simply is.
It is goodness, not because it follows rules, but because it exists as love itself.

Now, imagine yourself standing in a vast, open field.
Golden sunlight dances across the grass.
The air is fresh, crisp, alive.
In the distance, you hear the rhythmic beat of hooves against the earth.

A magnificent horse approaches.
Strong, free, and powerful, it moves with grace—unapologetic, untamed.
It does not ask for permission to run; it simply *knows* how to be.

This horse is your guide.
It embodies the essence of movement, integrity, and trust in life's natural flow.
Watch it now, breathing in its presence.
Feel the earth beneath your feet vibrating with its energy.

The horse bows its head, inviting you to come closer.
You reach out and place your hand against its warm coat.
Feel its steady breath, its pulse, its life force—unwavering, free, whole.

It asks you to ride with it.
Not to control it.
Not to restrain it.
But to trust it.

As you gentle climb on its back, you let go of the need to make everything right.
You do not have to direct every step.
You do not have to correct the path.
The horse *knows* the way.

And as it moves, you feel the wind rushing through you, carrying away old judgments,
The weight of perfection,
The fear of making mistakes.

Instead, there is only this moment.
This breath.
This freedom.

You and the horse move together as one—
A dance of trust, of rhythm, of pure being.

You are not defined by rigid lines.
You are not bound by impossible standards.
You are whole.
You are free.

Let that truth sink into your bones.
Feel it settle into your essence.
Breathe it in.

And when you are ready, gently bring your awareness back.
Back to your breath.
Back to the room around you.
Carrying this wisdom, this feeling, this connection with you.

And as you open your eyes, know this:
You are not here to fix the world.
You are here to *be* in it.
And that . . . is already enough.

Type 7—Writing Prompts

WILD ESSENCE FOR TYPE 1

1. RELEASING PERFECTION:

The horse moves with grace and freedom, unburdened by the need to be perfect. Reflect on a time when you allowed yourself to let go of control and simply enjoy the moment. How did it feel? How can you invite more of that ease into your life?

2. Compassion for Yourself:

Type 1s often hold themselves to high standards and can be their own harshest critics. Write a letter from your wisest, most compassionate self to the part of you that feels the need to be perfect. What would you say to remind yourself that you are already good enough?

3. Finding Joy in What Is:

The horse does not question whether it is doing life right—it simply moves forward with trust. Imagine if you released the belief that things had to be a certain way to be good enough. What parts of your life are already beautiful, just as they are? How can you allow yourself to fully appreciate them today?

Type 9—First Step

Guided Meditation for the Type 9:
Essence and the Bison

This meditation is designed to help the Enneagram Type 9 in you to connect with your true essence, beyond the need to merge, avoid conflict, or seek external harmony.

The bison, a symbol of strength, grounded presence, and deep inner peace, will guide you toward the realization that true peace comes not from avoiding, but from fully embodying yourself and your presence in the world.

Type 9—Bison

SETTLING INTO PRESENCE

Take a deep breath in . . . and exhale slowly.
Feel your body relax, your breath deepen, your mind soften.

There is nothing to fix in this moment.
Nothing to change.
Nothing to blend into.
Simply be here.

Bring your awareness to your heart.
At your very core, there is a steady, quiet light—your essence.
It is not defined by the needs of others.
It is not shaped by external harmony.
It simply is.

Whole. Rooted. Enough.

Breathe into this light . . .

Let it expand within you, gently filling the spaces
where you have made yourself small.
Where you have held back your voice.
Where you have stepped aside for the comfort of others.

You do not need to fade into the background.
You are meant to be fully here.

Now, imagine yourself standing in the middle of a vast, open plain.
Golden grass sways in the breeze, rolling out endlessly before you.
The sky stretches wide above you, open and endless.

There is stillness here,
Yet also deep movement,
A quiet, powerful rhythm of life itself.

You take a step forward,
Feeling the earth beneath your feet.
Strong. Steady. Unmoving.
This land supports you.
It welcomes you.

You belong here.

In the distance, a bison emerges.
Its massive form moves slowly, deliberately, with a presence that
commands respect.
It does not rush.
It does not force.
It simply is—rooted, steady, unshaken.

The bison meets your gaze,
And in its deep, dark eyes,
You see something you have always known:

You do not need to disappear to keep the peace.
Your presence is peace.
Not because you are silent,
But because you are fully here.

Let those words settle into your being.
Let go of the fear that taking up space will disrupt harmony.
Let go of the habit of fading into the background.
Let go of the belief that your voice is not needed.

Your presence matters.
Your truth matters.
You are not separate from life.
You are life.

The bison takes another step, and you follow.
Not to merge,
Not to escape,
But to walk fully in your own power.

The earth beneath your feet welcomes you.
The sky above you opens for you.
The world is not asking you to disappear.
It is asking you to be here.

You feel the weight of your own body,
The strength in your breath,
The depth of your presence.

You are not passive.
You are not invisible.
You are a force—steady, powerful, whole.

The bison pauses,
Turns to you one last time,

Then lowers its great head in quiet recognition.

It sees you.
And you see yourself.

No more hiding.
No more blending in.
No more waiting for permission to exist fully.

You belong—as you are.

Breathe deeply.
Feel your body, your presence, your power.

Slowly, bring your awareness back.
Back to your breath.
Back to this moment.

And as you open your eyes,
Know this truth:

You are not separate.
You are not small.
You are fully here.
And the world is better because of it.

Type 9—Writing Prompts

WILD ESSENCE FOR TYPE 9

1. HONORING YOUR VOICE:

The bison stands firm, fully present in its own power. Reflect on a time when you spoke up for yourself or took a stand for something that mattered to you. How did it feel? What would it be like to trust that your voice and presence truly matter?

2. Embracing Your Full Presence:

Type 9s often merge with others to maintain peace, sometimes losing sight of their own desires. If there were no external expectations or conflicts to avoid, what would you truly want for yourself? Describe a life where you move forward with clarity and purpose.

3. Moving with Intention:

The bison does not rush or hesitate—it moves with steady, grounded confidence. Write about an area in your life where you feel stuck or hesitant to take action. What is one small but meaningful step you could take today to move forward with purpose?

Type 8—First Step

Guided Meditation for the Type 8:
Essence and the Mountain Lion

This meditation is designed to help the Enneagram Type 8 in you connect with your true essence, beyond the need for control, strength, or protection.

The mountain lion, a symbol of power, courage, and self-mastery, will guide you toward the realization that true strength comes not from force, but from presence, wisdom, and trust in yourself.

Type 8—Mountain Lion

SETTLING INTO STILLNESS

Take a deep breath in . . . and exhale slowly.
Feel your body settle, your muscles soften, your breath deepen.

You are safe here.
There is nothing to protect.
Nothing to fight.
Nothing to prove.

With each inhale, you gather presence.
With each exhale, you release tension.

Bring your awareness to your heart.
At your core, there is a steady, powerful light—your essence.
It is not defined by how strong you appear.
It is not measured by how much you control.
It simply is.

Whole. Grounded. Unshaken.

Breathe into this light . . .
Let it expand within you, softening any resistance,
Releasing any need to defend.

You do not need to hold this moment in your grip.
It is already yours.

Now, imagine yourself standing at the base of a vast mountain.
The air is crisp, the ground solid beneath your feet.
The wind moves around you, but you stand firm—
Rooted. Strong. Present.

This mountain is not an obstacle.
It is not a challenge to conquer.
It is a reflection of your own power—steady, timeless, unmovable.

You take a step forward, feeling the strength in your body,
Not from force,
Not from resistance,
But from the deep knowing that you belong here.

A presence stirs in the distance.
From the rocky cliffs above, a mountain lion watches you.
Its golden eyes are clear, unshaken, piercing through illusion.

It does not attack.
It does not retreat.
It simply knows itself.

The mountain lion moves toward you with effortless grace,
Every step purposeful, every movement powerful.
Not because it dominates—
But because it trusts itself completely.

The lion pauses before you,
Looking deep into your soul,
And without words, it speaks:

True strength is not in control.
True power is in presence.
You do not need to force.
You do not need to prove.
You already are.

Let those words settle into your being.
Let go of the need to always be strong.
Let go of the fear that vulnerability is weakness.
Let go of the belief that you must always lead the charge.

Your power is not in domination.
Your power is in being fully yourself.

The mountain lion turns,
Walking up the ridge,
Moving through the terrain with ease,
Fearless, unburdened.

And you follow.
Not chasing.
Not forcing.
Simply moving with life, instead of against it.

There is nothing to prove here.
Nothing to guard against.
Only the deep, steady confidence
Of knowing who you are.

The mountain lion reaches the peak and stands,
Looking out over the vast expanse of land below.

You stand beside it,
Breathing in the view,
Feeling the stillness of power that needs no explanation.

You do not have to push to be strong.
You do not have to fight to be respected.
Your presence alone is enough.

The mountain lion bows its head slightly,
Not as submission,
But as recognition.

It sees you.
And you see yourself.

Take a deep breath in . . . and exhale.
Feel your body, your heart, your presence—whole and unshaken.

Slowly, bring your awareness back.
Back to your breath.
Back to your body.
Back to this moment.

And when you open your eyes,
Know this truth:

You are strong.
You are powerful.
You are enough—without having to prove it.

Type 8—Writing Prompts

WILD ESSENCE FOR TYPE 8

1. THE STRENGTH OF VULNERABILITY:
The mountain lion moves with quiet confidence, knowing that true strength does not come from force, but from trust in oneself. Reflect on a time when you allowed yourself to be open, vulnerable, or emotionally honest. How did it feel? What did you learn about your own strength in that moment?

2. Letting Go of the Battle:
Type 8s often move through life with a sense of needing to be strong and in control. Imagine a world where you don't have to fight or prove anything—where you are safe to simply be. How would that change the way you show up in your relationships and daily life?

3. Trusting Others, Trusting Yourself:
The mountain lion knows when to act and when to rest. Write

about a time when you allowed yourself to trust someone fully, without feeling the need to be in control. How did it feel? How can you create more space for trust, both in yourself and in others?

Returning to Essence

Essence

At the core of the Enneagram lies not just knowledge, but a call to return—return to who we have always been beneath the fears, longings, and defenses we've carried.

The Enneagram is more than a system of personality; it is a path of remembering. It illuminates the ways we have learned to survive, the ways we have sought safety, love, and meaning, and the ways we can begin to release what no longer serves us.

Each type holds a journey, a path shaped by seeking something outside of ourselves, only to realize that what we were searching for was within us all along.

The Head Types (7,6,5) navigate the world through thought, seeking knowledge, security, and freedom, believing that understanding will bring them the certainty they crave. And yet, their greatest wisdom is found not in certainty, but in presence. True clarity, trust, and joy are not found in the mind's endless seeking, but in learning to rest in the moment, embracing life as it unfolds.

The Heart Types (4,3,2) live through the language of emotion, seeking love, significance, and authenticity, believing that they must be something more to be worthy. And yet, their deepest realization is that they have always belonged, that their worth is not earned through giving, achieving, or being unique—it is already within them, unshakable and radiant.

The Gut Types (1,9,8) move through life with instinct as their compass, seeking control, autonomy, and integrity, believing that they must shape the world around them to find their place. And yet, their greatest strength lies not in force or resistance, but in trusting their own being, standing firmly in their presence, and knowing that they are whole, without the need to push or pull.

Throughout *Wild Essence: Enneagram Meditations Through Animal Spirits*, the hummingbird, great blue heron, owl, koi, whale, dolphin, horse, bison, and mountain lion have stood as guides—not as something to chase, but as reflections of what already lives within us. These animals do not seek to justify their existence. They do not ask permission to be. They do not hesitate to take up space or to follow the natural rhythms of life.

- And the hummingbird whispers that joy is not something to chase—it is found in the fullness of now.
- The great blue heron reveals that steadiness is not found in certainty, but in trusting our own balance.
- The owl calls us to let go of over-analysis and trust the wisdom that already resides within.
- The koi reminds us that there is nothing missing within us; we are already whole.
- The whale teaches us that we do not have to prove our worth; we are already vast, already enough.
- The dolphin shows us that love is not something we must earn—it is something we already are.

- The horse carries us toward freedom, not through control, but through trust in the journey.
- The bison reminds us that we are not separate from life— we are deeply rooted within it.
- The mountain lion teaches us that true strength is not in dominance, but in presence.

We have spent our lives running toward something—control, love, knowledge, peace—only to realize that we are not meant to chase life, but to experience it fully.

The Enneagram is not a map that tells you who to be—it is a mirror reflecting who you already are. You are not incomplete. You are not lacking. You are already whole.

This journey is not about becoming someone new; it is about remembering who you have always been.

May you walk forward with presence.
May you stand firm in your essence.
May you trust that you are already enough.

And may you always know that no matter how far you wander, your true self is always waiting to welcome you home.

Wendy Van de Poll, MS, CEOL
January 17, 2025

Wild Essence Enneagram Certification

If you would like to be added to the mailing list to get notified when this program will begin please sign up here:
https://wendyvandepoll.com/wild-essence-enneagram-certification

or

https://enneagramofessence.com/wild-essence

TAUGHT BY:

Tammy Hendrix, LCSW—https://enneagramofessence.com
and
Wendy Van de Poll, MS, CEOL—https://wendyvandepoll.com

Acknowledgments

With deep reverence, I offer my gratitude to the spirit guides of the Enneagram. These timeless guides illuminate the hidden pathways within me. Their wisdom reveals not just who I am, but who I have always been beneath my fears, patterns, and longings.

They remind me that transformation is not about becoming something new, but about returning to the essence that has always been there.

I also honor the voices of the animals, the sacred messengers who walk beside me in silence yet speak in ways the soul understands every day. Their presence whispers of strength, trust, freedom, and belonging, teaching me what it means to move through life with instinct, heart, and presence.

I want to express my deepest gratitude to Tammy Hendrix for her incredible guidance and wisdom on my journey with the Enneagram. Her insights, compassion, and deep understanding have profoundly shaped my growth, helping me see myself and others with greater clarity and kindness. Tammy's generosity in sharing her knowledge has been a true gift, and I am endlessly grateful for the impact she has had on my appreciation of this transformative system. Thank you, Tammy —you are truly fantastic!

May the Enneagram and the spirit of these animals continue to awaken, heal, and guide me back to my true

About the Author

Wendy Van de Poll is a professionally certified Enneagram practitioner, animal medium, and bestselling author who bridges the wisdom of the Enneagram with the profound messages of the animal world.

As a pioneer in animal communication and intuitive pet grief support, she has devoted her life to deepening the connection between humans and animals, both in this world and beyond.

Through her work, Wendy helps individuals explore the Enneagram's transformative power, guiding them to connect with the spirit and wisdom of animals. As a tested animal communicator and medium, she receives and shares messages from animals, helping people find clarity, healing, and deeper self-awareness through their relationships with the natural world.

Her approach is deeply compassionate and intuitive, offering a safe and sacred space for those seeking guidance—not only in navigating the grief of pet loss but also in uncovering their own true essence through the Enneagram. She believes that animals hold a unique mirror to our souls, teaching us lessons of instinct, presence, and unconditional love.

Wendy holds a Master of Science degree in wolf ecology and behavior and has had the rare experience of running with wild wolves in Minnesota, observing coyotes in Massachusetts, and forming close bonds with the foxes in her own backyard.

In addition to her work as an Enneagram practitioner and animal medium, Wendy is a grief and end-of-life coach for pets and their people, an intuitive mentor, and a publishing coach for those looking to share their own journeys.

Her bestselling books, live events, and online programs provide wisdom, insight, and healing, empowering individuals to navigate grief, self-discovery, and the profound bond between humans and animals.

You can reach her at https://www.wendyvandepoll.com or www.center forpetlossgriefcom/contact.

Also by Wendy Van de Poll

Pet Bereavement Series

My Dog Is Dying: What Do I Do?
My Dog Has Died: What Do I Do?

My Cat Is Dying: What Do I Do?
My Cat Has Died: What Do I Do?

Healing a Child's Pet Loss Grief

The Pet Professional's Guide to Pet Loss

Pet Loss Poem Books

Pet Loss Poems: To Heal Your Heart and Soul
Pet Loss Poems: For Those Who Loved a Cat
Pet Loss Poems: For Those Who Loved a Dog

Human-Animal Books

Animal Wisdom: Conversations From The Heart Between Animals and Their People

Free Book

Healing Your Heart From Pet Loss Grief

Children's Picture Books

The Adventures of Ms. Addie Pants Series

The Rescue

The Ice Storm

New Friends

Off to School

Paranormal Cozy Mysteries (a.k.a. Melanie Snow)

Witch's Tail

Howl Play

Tail of a Feather

Impossible Mischief

Pawtrayal

TO RECEIVE NOTIFICATION WHEN MORE BOOKS ARE PUBLISHED, PLEASE GO TO:

https://centerforpetlossgrief.com or https://wendyvandepoll.com.

We will add you to the mailing list after you
download your free gift.

www.ingramcontent.com/pod-product-compliance
Lightning Source LLC
Chambersburg PA
CBHW032118280326
41933CB00009B/896